Before I Die, I Must Say This

Michael Tavon

Amazon Self-Publishing
Kindle Direct Publishing

© 2022 by Michael Tavon

All rights reserved, including the rights to reproduce this book or portions thereof in any form whatsoever.

All contents are original works by author Michael Tavon, any redistribution without the author's consent illegal

Posting any content from this book without crediting the author is considered plagiarism.

Before I Die, I Must Say This

Other Works by The Author

Fiction

God is a Woman
Far From Heaven

Poetry

Don't Wait til I Die to Love Me II
The Pisces
Songs for Each Mood II
Don't Wait Til I Die to Love Me
Nirvana: Pieces of Self-Healing vol. 1 & 2
Young Heart, Old Soul
Songs for Each Mood
A Day Without Sun

Collabs w/ Moonsoulchild

Self-Talks
Heal, Inspire, Love

Michael Tavon

Follow the Author

Tiktok: MichaelTavon
Instagram: ByMichaelTavon
Twitter: MichaelTavon

Follow the illustrator

Instagram: 2dwoe

Before I Die, I Must Say This

Table of Contents:

Section I: Too Deep for The Intro

(TW: rape culture, addiction, and abuse)

Section II: Before I Die

Section III: I Must Say This

Michael Tavon

Dear Reader,

Read this book with an open mind. I know poetry has the power to connect us through words, and most poetry lovers read poetry because they see a reflection of themselves in it. Keep this in mind; all poetry isn't meant to be relatable to you. Some poems are written to help you see a worldview outside your own. Poetry will open your eyes world you're foreign to when you give it a chance. So, when you read poems you don't relate to, don't dismiss them as *not good*, and don't fall into the trap of believing all relatable poems *are good*. With that said, I hope you enjoy this collection because it will be my last poetry book for a very long time.

P.S, In this collection introduce a new form of poem called *Prism*.

Before I Die, I Must Say This

Before I Die, I Must Say This

Michael Tavon

Before I Die, I Must Say This

Section I: Too Deep For The Intro

Michael Tavon

Before I Die, I Must Say This

Flowers

Today, I will give myself the flowers I deserve.
I'm too impatient to wait for them to be handed to me.

Orchids often die before
 they're given to someone alive
and roses of many hues are used to decorate
 more tombstones than celebrations.

So, instead of waiting,
 I will give myself a bouquet today
I dare anyone to try to pry them
from my fucking hands.

I deserve my flowers now, not when I die.

Michael Tavon

Heirloom

When cycles skip like a broken record,
trauma becomes a family heirloom
Of despair and vices

Vice gripped by the past,
Pain latches to the bloodline
With a cold burn, like dry ice

Ice cubes floating in a
Cognac pool was how the men
in my family drowned their agony

Agony formed who they are,
I strive to break the mold
That shaped my family

My family's heirloom
Won't be passed down
To my children

My children,
Will be the manifestation
Of my healing

Before I Die, I Must Say This

To the Loved on Who Struggle with Addiction

It hurts to see someone I love
lose themselves.

Then I fear the possibility
Of you never rediscovering
Who you used to be.

Your addiction isn't my burden

Yet somehow I keep wondering
Where did I go wrong?
How did I miss the signs for so long

I hate myself for not being more responsible,
Since I love you, I'm responsible for you, right?

You're grown,
you make your own damn choices
Somehow, I blame myself.

It hurts me, as much as it hurts you
Is what some parents would say
before breaking their child

In this case,
This hurts me more
than it hurts you
As you break me,
And the ones who love you

You live.

Michael Tavon

Under the influence, blissfully
While this sober heart
Beats heavy with worry

Because seeing you lose yourself
Means there's a chance
 you may never find your way back

Before I Die, I Must Say This

Eulogy (From Me 2 U)

To those who mourn my demise
Although my time on earth has expired
This isn't a goodbye,
My soul will rise high to a friendly sky
After I'm planted 6 feet deep
So don't weep for too long
Reprise my life like a spiritual song,
Life goes on,
I'm where I belong,
With earth, The mother
Who has given so much since birth
I'm giving my bones and flesh in return
A fair trade.

Here's my final message to you:

I hope our time together was worth
Every second spent,
I hope I created more laugh lines
Than headaches
Concrete souls, our eternal bond
Written in cement
In case I didn't say I love you
Before it was too late

Hear me now - I love you
With every piece of fabric
My heart was threaded
Unravel my layers,

Michael Tavon

You'll see your reflection
I would not have
Grown into what I became,
To you I'm indebted,

Each of you
played an instrumental
part of my outcome
If life is music,
You helped me create
One hell of an album,

Promise that you will sing about me

I love you
I thank you
I love you
I thank you
I can't express it enough

Take this last nugget of gold before I go:

When the final grains of sand
Trickle down in your hourglass,
The money you amass - won't matter,
Your vanity will be swept into the past
The only green that remains is grass,
Earth will still spin when your clock stops
How you made others feel
will be the legacy that lasts

I hope,
I shifted the mountains inside of you
I hope,
I planted enough seeds

Before I Die, I Must Say This

to help gardens bloom

I hope,
you celebrate me more than you mourn
A vessel I became
the day I was born

I hope my life was defined with purpose,
I'd be hurt if my time
Was perceived as worthless
Before leaving the earth's surface

We are children
Of the sun & moon.
I was truly blessed to share
this beautiful home with you

Promise to take care
While I'm gone

Michael Tavon

Museum

When the casket becomes
 my final resting space
 don't host a funeral in my honor
they're too slow and bleak

build a museum,
with exhibits of my mistakes
and displays of my pain

Hire Morgan Freeman as the tour
guide, trust me, he will still be alive

So, he can share my life story
with the youth as scattered memories
From my preserved brain
Projects 3D images
So they can relive each
moment with me

my glasses, desk, and laptop
will be artifacts
for the guests
to view life from my perspective

I loathe funerals,
Honor my life with a museum instead

Before I Die, I Must Say This

Grandpa's Cancer

His lugs & liver –shriveled and dark
like dried prunes
After decades of burning newports
and swigging liquor

With cancer spreading like wildfire
In his body
The doctor said grandpa
had six months to live
and advised the smoking
and drinking to cease
If he wanted the chance to see
as many moons as possible

Grandpa knew sobriety & cancer
Were two losing battles
so his lips continued to suck from
cigarette butts & bottle mouths

as time waned, cancer slowly changed
the grumpy old drunk
into a man who
shared his toothless smile
and sung gospel songs,

he told jokes and stories from his youth
the good man - once buried
six feet deep in depression
reemerged to the surface
to show us the life that would've been

Michael Tavon

if he were free from his burdens
he stopped flashing his pistol
at family functions

the cancer festering inside
reminded him how precious family is

Six months lasted for three years
He smoked & drank
Til the day his body retired

Momma said:
He died peacefully,
After 74 years of hardship & regrets
He was finally able to set himself free
when his wife & children had forgiven him
Most of all, he had forgiven himself

Before I Die, I Must Say This

Big Brother

The big brother
Of two beautiful sisters

The yesterdays of our
Youth still seems fresh like mango
dangling from the trees
we used to pick
I still remember,
The day they were freshly baked
From momma's oven
So soft & warm
As I cradled them
In my arms

I became a big brother at 5
And again at 11

Momma said:
treat women the way
I want boys to treat them

Poppa showed me how to
Protect my sisters from guys
Like him

I wanted to be their sky,
Someone they could look up to
So, when it rained
They could still see
the silver lining
in my grey clouds

Michael Tavon

Time seems like an illusion
The way they bloomed
before my very eyes

One has a heart purer than gold
And made me an uncle
To a handsome baby boy

The other,
Lights up every room she enters
And sets fire to every stage
She steps on

I'm so proud of who
They've become

Three hearts, one home
No matter how far we are
We will never be alone

Before I Die, I Must Say This

Mother's Depression

I didn't understand why
 mommas' eyes became islands,
When no one was around

 oblivious as to why
her blanket wrapped
her body tight like a cocoon
as she slept all noon,
maybe she wanted to bloom
into a butterfly too

As a child,
I never understood why mom & dad
Hardly, settled in the same room
The two lived separate lives
under the same roof

I was too naïve to see
Mom's blood boiling
When dad chose the homies
over comin' home
to his wife & son

When I grew up,
I understood why she cried

The Huxtables

My parents were the best for their children,
but the worst for each other

They were my 101 courses to love,

As a kid, I thought
Getting drunk, fussing,
Stressing over bills,
and coming home as I pleased
was the best a relationship could get

I always admired The Cosby Show
And imagined
my parents as the Huxtable's

When I asked my mom *"why can't you and dad
be more like Clair & Cliff."*

She said, "marriages like that aren't real."
That was a straight bullet to my faith,

For a long time, I believed -
Love was synonymous with distance
Marriage was tied to pain
Clair and cliff were a myth
And there's no such thing
as true happiness,
Just a lifetime of settling for less

My parents weren't
the best example of marriage
That's why I always
dreamed of being a Huxtable

Before I Die, I Must Say This

Carry on Tradition

Grandpa wore the scent
 Of hard alcohol like cologne
  'til the day he died

My uncles abused their livers
  With cheap liquor 'til this very day
  My aunt walked
  Drunk even when sober,

& I've never seen
  My father, turn down a bottle
  Or tall can.
  Beer is his morning coffee

Alcoholism runs deep in my blood,
  It's inevitable. I knew
   the torch would someday
  be passed down to me

When I took my first swig at age ten
 It felt like a rite of passage

My uncles looked proud
  When they cheered and said
  "put some hair on yo chest, boy."
  As Budweiser flushed down my throat.

After grandpa died,
  I knew alcohol abuse was nothing
  To glorify

Michael Tavon

Prism: My Makers

Love,
Never lived
Between my parents
Silver cuffs as wedding bands
Their bed, a lonely jail cell for two

Love,
Was a myth
An ugly romance
They said 'I do' way too fast
Divorce was a sweet celebration

Love,
My parents
Never learned how to
Speak with kind words, only fists,
silence and slurs, marriage was a curse

Before I Die, I Must Say This

Blood is Thicker

They say:

Blood is thicker than water,

But Both feels the same
With eyes closed shut
So who do you trust
When push comes to shove?

Blood will leave you homeless
Over a ten-year grudge
Sometimes,
All you got in common is blood
What flows through your veins
Isn't sacred, it's inevitable
blood will double-cross you
Blood isn't always safe
Blood doesn't know you
As well as water does

Water runs deeper than blood
When water doesn't drown you
It helps you stay afloat

Who do you trust
Water or blood?
You'll never know
Until it's time for them to show up

Michael Tavon

Momma's Second Husband

I came out of my room,
To the scene of him pinning
My mother to the couch
With a fist cocked and loaded

I've never heard so much fear
In my mother's voice,
She screamed for help

The crucifix hanging on the wall
Became a baseball bat
As I prayed to Jesus
To spare some mercy for what
was coming

I swung at his head like a fastball
- It felt so damn good when I hit
A home run,

Before he knew what hit him
My arm wrapped around his neck
Like a serpent

The blood from his gash
Smeared on my t-shirt

At that moment, I didn't want air to
Enter his lungs; he didn't deserve to breathe

He scratched & clawed
To free himself
But my arm was made of steel

Before I Die, I Must Say This

I unloaded my other first
To his pale face,
My mother cried,
"stop before you kill him."

I released the drunken fool
From my grip,
He gasped for air
Like he was trying to recoup
all breaths he lost

A flood of tears,
Rushed from my eyes
I drowned in my sorrow
~anger came over me like rain

My mother tried to comfort me
While he looked confused
And asked,
"Why the fuck is he crying?"
"Because he's not an animal like you."
She said

"I'm so sorry," I cried.
Even in my most violent state
My heart had a soft spot

For the first time,
I saw what my rage could do,
My heart tore in half
When I realized how dangerous
I could be when
Someone tries to hurt
Someone I Love

Michael Tavon

The 20s

My 20s were buried
6 feet deep
In a casket of gold
A beautiful way to exit
This ugly world
Now,
30 lives with the grief
of having to let go so young
And being forced to grow old
As the essence of adolescence
Leaves my body
I live in new flesh,
Growing up is inevitable
Time waits for no one
We either move with it
Or get left in the past

Before I Die, I Must Say This

Duplex: Mommas 'Type'

Her 2nd husband was fascinated with booze
Just like my father - My mother has a type

My mother's type- homesick when sober,
They felt at home when drunk

They stayed at home when drunk
The same place my mother was raised

A drunk raised my mother
He showed affection by striking his fists

The fists of my mother's husbands
would say *I love you* before putting her to sleep

She slept alone, the same way her mother did.
My mother's husbands loved booze more than marriage

She attracted men who loved booze,
Just like her father - my mom has a type

Michael Tavon

A Letter to Those Who Love Me

When anxiety raced through my heart and crippled my ability to move forward, you didn't bail on me, Nah not at all. Instead, you remained by my side and provided a shoulder to lean on.

When clouds of self-doubt rained inside my mind, you didn't give up on me; you reminded me of the sun that shines within you me when my days are dull. You connected the stars in my heart to form a constellation when I felt lost at night.

When my decisions didn't align with your advice, you didn't say 'I told you so' when I was wrong. It was a lesson I needed to learn. You remained my biggest fan through thick and thin. Despite my mistakes, you still cheered for me to win.

You kept me grounded when my head was stuck in the clouds. You never pushed me away, nor did you kick dirt in my face when I fell on my face. I know it wasn't always easy, so thank you for being patient with me.

Before I Die, I Must Say This

POV

I take compliments the way I avoid
secondhand smoke –

I pause my breath, trying not to offend
the person blowing air in my space

I choke on my breath when
words of kindness get attached to my name

despite feeling unworthy, some compliments
remain tattooed on my heart

The creases around my mouth remind me
Of the times I've heard, "your smile brightens my day."

The rip currents that spread from my shoulders
tell the story of every time
My arms stretched oceanwide
to protect a loved one from drowning
with a warm hug.

And the callouses on my palms
Are rewards for every time a reader
Encouraged me to *never quit writing*
Or said, *'your words saved my life.'*

Sometimes, compliments shed light
 On the beauty of your flaws

Michael Tavon

<u>Prism: Musical Chairs</u>

Home,
Changed like clothes
We always packed boxes
Moving - suburbs to ghettos
New beginnings weren't always lovely

Home,
Where roaches
Were stubborn like mules
And refused to leave
When they took over, we packed again

Home,
A poem
Of dead metaphors
Scribed on eviction letters
I dreamed of haikus; home was free verse

Before I Die, I Must Say This

My Last Name

I look nothing like my last name
Because my last name
doesn't belong to me,

I lived a lifetime
carrying the namesake of roots
My ancestors' blood didn't help spread
Across the land

This last name was forced upon them,
Then passed down to me

my father's blood
stained the soil of Arkansas
My mother's blood
Was born in Georgia
But my last name traveled
from Ireland
and found its way
to my family

This last name lives with us
Like a freeloader

This name looks nothing like us
But claims to be related
Our blood doesn't match this name

Michael Tavon

Yet, we continue to claim
Who we are not
With no shame

I know where this last name
Came from
Sadly, I know
Nothing about my own

Before I Die, I Must Say This

How Many R.Kelly's Do You Know: Duplex

No one calls the cops on the older cousin
Who recruits high school girls
But they call the girls fast

Young girls get attracted to the fast life
When no one is around to protect them

Who's there to protect the little boy
when his family swears he's crying wolf

The only wolf he fears is the one
Sleeping in his momma's bed

Momma's bed holds a predator
Who roams when his prey
prays for protection

A prayer that never comes true
Becomes a broken promise from God

God's promises become broken the moment
Pastor uses his praying hands
to touch a little girl's sacred areas

There's a fine line between sacred
and scarred for life

Too many children, scarred for life
Because no one calls the cops
When the predator is someone they know

Michael Tavon

My Name is My Name

Everybody knows a few
Of us
But I carry my name
The way a mother cradles her newborn –
Proud & Gentle

My mother
Swollen and starved for rest
Didn't have enough time to create
A name to define me
So she settled
For my father's name
And prayed I would never
Grow into another him.
"You're just like yo damn daddy,"
She'd curse me. when angry."

My name is a manifestation of everything
she didn't want me to be.

I grew up admiring the men,
Who made my name synonymous
With greatness,
As I aspired to find my place
Amongst them

My name - worn down
to the last thread –
out of style - played out,
The new generation
call it vintage

Before I Die, I Must Say This

I'm proud,
to have a name, too crowded
and still found a way to stand out

Michael Tavon

Pep: Neighborhood Superstar

Pep — is what his loyal customers
Called him.
My cousin, the local chef,
the neighborhood chemist, in the kitchen

Crack fiends approach the window
Like a drive-thru
He served crack rock fixes
Fresh from the kitchen
His name became a legend -
A local superstar
In strip clubs
I wore his expensive hand-me-downs
With pride

He'd often count
his earnings on my bed,
And give me the wrinkled dollar bills
So I didn't have to wait in the free lunch
Line in school

Pep told me not to follow his example
That my future was brighter than his.
Pep must be a prophet too,
Because his foresight was right

Before I Die, I Must Say This

Bullet Tag

The crackling sound pierces
the air like fireworks,
My curious eyes peek out the window
Small explosions of light,
Flash amid the dark alley
We duck for cover,
We pray for hot shells
Not to find us.
Round for round,
A game of hide and seek
We can't afford to lose
The taggers chase and shoot
Until a bullet finds home base,
Inside homeboy's body,
Another life claimed
In this bloody game of bullet tag

Michael Tavon

Nerf Wars

Who knew,
Shooting Nerf guns & super-soakers
In the backyard
Was foreshadowing for
Black boys starting
Wars over turf that's not ours
Tagging bodies with bullets
Not made of Styrofoam,
Leaving too many tees
Soaked in blood instead of water

Some boys didn't rush to grow up
They played with toy guns
until they too old to play

Other boys grew bored of the toys
With their trigger fingers
Still itchin'
And started blasting real guns
At other boys
Who resemble them

Before I Die, I Must Say This

Missing Person's Report

Women and children go missing
The way deadbeat fathers do ~
Without trace & void of closure.
Leaving families to mend
Parts of their broken home
As they spend cold tears like dollar bills
grief - collects its debt
One way or another
Broken families hope
one day they won't have
to miss the person they love anymore
The world's saddest game
of hide n seek
Some victims never make it back home
Like deadbeats-
The exit of a loved one
Is something a family
Never fully heals from

Michael Tavon

Prism: Family BBQ's

Drunk,
My father
Was light on his feet
As happy as he could be
Always the life of the barbeque

Drunk,
The O.G's
Played spades until dark
2pac's songs echoed the hood
As grill & weed smoke signaled, the air

Drunk,
My aunt was
Kissing her girlfriend
As the men said slurs & jokes
Liquor and gaycism don't mix too well

Drunk,
My grandpa
Was at every party
Cussing and waving his gun
When he stumbled, the fun was over

Drunk,
The lone way
My fam could function
Together in the same space
Until alcohol tore them apart

Before I Die, I Must Say This

They Never Said I Love You

My parents never said
I love you to each other
But they yelled *fuck you*
Like it was a contest
To see who could scream it louder

My parents
couldn't tell you what color
the other's eyes are,
they still look away
when they speak.

My parents never *hugged,*
kissed, or held hands
I've witnessed sworn
enemies show more affection

The couple who never said, "I love you."
Somehow, planted
three beautiful lives onto this earth

When people say, "Anything's possible."
I laugh to myself and think
"How'd you think I got here in the first place?"

My parents proved,
roses can grow from concrete

Michael Tavon

Someone I Miss

Dear grandpa,
The scent of Newport smoke
still lingers in the room you left behind
your bed is dressed neatly

like its waiting for you to rest
your tired body after a long day
of watching Tom and Jerry &
sipping brews

Sundays no longer
feel the same without you
Cursing at the tv when the Dallas Cowboys
made an awful play
You'd shout so hard
The phlegm in your chest
Rattled like dice in a hand,
My stomach turned
Every time you'd spit it into your
Tin can

your old school Lincoln
became a statue in your parking spot
until the city took it away
Don't worry, no one
Changed the country station

O, how you loved country
Tunes so much you threatened to
"shoot the mothafucka."

Before I Die, I Must Say This

Who dared to change it

By the way, tell Kobe I said hey
Watching the Lakers haven't
Been the same
Since you both faded away

And the house no longer feels hotter
Than the oven on Thanksgiving
When I enter, the thermostat often turns
Like the earth you're buried in,
When you were here
You'd refuse to use the A.C
You were afraid of the bills
Going 'sky high
So we'd sweat in our sleep
Every summer night

By now, you've realized
Much hasn't changed
Except for the fact our family
Stopped feeling like family
Since the day
Your casket dropped

Michael Tavon

Mama's Headaches

I gave my momma
her fair share of headaches
With all the sarcastic remarks
Forgetting to take the frozen chicken out
And staying out after dark
But she never took a day off
from loving me

My younger sister,
Gave momma her fair
share of headaches too
With the lies & sneaking around
Turning off her phone,
Disappearing for hours at a time
She never took a day off from loving her

My baby sister gave my momma
her fair share of migraines,
Her lazy ways, back talking
sneaking back into the house
before the sun woke up
she still never took a day off
from loving her

Being a mother is a full-time job
With no pay raise or 401k plan,
mother never quit on us
Nor took a day off
Despite how difficult
Being a mother is

Before I Die, I Must Say This

The Scar on My Arm

I was twelve years young -
Hormones racing like horsepower

With traveling eyes & two hands
Desperate to explore
Places they weren't invited to

We were in sewing class,
Where we were taught
Not to play around with sharp objects

homeboy tapped my shoulder and said
"I bet you won't grab her booty."

She stood,
with a blade in her hand
Cutting fabric,
Minding her business

I went over & grabbed
something that didn't belong to me
My palm copped its first feel

"Stop before I cut you."
She said with a smile on her face,
The blade held by her relaxed wrist

I took it as a sign to do it again
When she turned her back to me

Michael Tavon

I cuffed her cheek
In my palm
Like I was holding gold

"I told you to stop!"
Her hair slapped my face
As she turned around

I laughed,
and reached for a hug

She seemed
more afraid than angry

"I'm so sorry," she said.
"Sorry for what?"

My eyes were so high; I didn't realize
The blade sliced through
My flesh like a glazed ham

The pain didn't hit until
I saw my white meat
Dripping crimson from my skin
Like a broken shower head

The maintenance man
Poured drowned the gash
With rubbing alcohol
I held my tears back
The way I should've

Before I Die, I Must Say This

Held my hand
From touching her

The scar on my arm
Is a reminder
Of the last time I touched
A girl against her will

Michael Tavon

Definition/

Noun:
A Boosie:
/uh buuzy/

a man who upholds
Strong views against gay men and advocates for young boys to get sexually assaulted by older women to prove their Heterosexuality.
Ex: he was raised by A Boosie; that's why you shouldn't trust him.

Verb: past tense/ *Boosied*,
present tense/ *Boosing*

displaying a proud sense of predatory behavior & homophobia

Ex: He *boosied* his son when he was 12; the woman was 32.

He was *boosing* at the pride parade, Idk why he even attends.

Before I Die, I Must Say This

Boosie Badaszz Is A Trash Human

Somewhere in the ghetto
a little boy is getting
raped into the manhood,
He isn't ready for
A Boosie tells him passing through
a woman's legs are a rite of passage
And the sooner, the better

Jewish boys get Bar Mitzvahs
The little black boy gets a working girl
or stripper, hired by a Boosie
to turn that boy into a man

The little boy - unprotected,
In more ways than one
A Boosie auctions off his virginity
the way masters did slaves

The woman finds charm in
Introducing him
To a feeling far beyond his years

The little boy thinks rape is pleasure.
And sex is a transaction

The Boosie's he idolizes are predators
Who will groom him to become a Boosie too

Michael Tavon

The scariest thing about Boosie is the millions of men who think like him and the thousands of young boys who look up to them.

Before I Die, I Must Say This

Section II: I Must Say This

People Like You II

People like you understand how pain feels when it's fresh like the scent of rain because you've healed yourself after getting hurt time and time again.

Knowing what it is like sleep with an aching heart, you do everything in your power to ensure you are never the reason for someone's tears to fall.

People like you are too thoughtful to a fault because you often put others' needs before your peace, without a second thought.

You're brave for loving hard despite your heart getting torn apart. You're never afraid to move on; you believe in fresh starts.

Some people think you're a fool
For putting your all into a world
That doesn't appreciate you

That's far from true
I think the world needs more people like you

Before I Die, I Must Say This

I'm Not Okay

To say, "I'm not okay."
Is not a sign of weakness

you've been at war with yourself
for so long - you're still not easily broken
You deserve to unravel,
And explore the soft layers inside you

I know you don't want
to feel like a burden,
To those who adore you

But "I'm not okay,"
Is a declaration of reclaiming your power,
You're not a coward
Telling the truth
is the bravest act any hero could do

Let those words,
Become a safe space -
They don't have to be a prison

Say, 'I'm Not Okay."
With pride
Never pump your heart
With shame
For not being okay.

Michael Tavon

Unexpected Guest

When trauma comes knocking
Open the door, invite them in.

Show some hospitality,
Offer a drink

Trauma often pays a visit
To see how far you've come
And to remind you,
How much further you must travel
To find your peace

Trauma is frightening,
But insightful
Listen with intent
When it speaks to you
Set your anger to the side,
Hold a dialogue,
You'll learn so much more
About your past and present self
It's time to confront your trauma
Ignoring it won't fix
what's broken inside you

when trauma comes knocking
Treat your guest well

Before I Die, I Must Say This

Your trauma will tell you the
Words you need to hear
Even when you're too stubborn
To listen

Michael Tavon

The Tenant & The Owner

I've always been a worrier,
Anxiety has made a home out of me
And it's grown too cozy
within the depths of my soul

I never welcomed him
As a guest
But, I don't possess
the courage to tell him
to get the fuck out of my house
I live in constant stress
As he carelessly kicks
Dirt on my couch

I don't know what's it like
to live on my own
I figured it's best to deal
with his shit than to be alone

I've always been a worrier,
Anxiety occupies a room rent-free
My body is his home; I just own it

Some days,
he takes up the entire space
And I sleep outside

Sometimes when I smile
it's a façade to the chaos
Dwelling inside

Before I Die, I Must Say This

Duplex: Window Shopper

There's the life you have
Then there's the life you dream of

   You dream of this life
   That looks so gorgeous
   from the outside looking in

from the outside looking in
There's a price you can't afford

   You can't afford to pay out of pocket,
   What are you willing to sacrifice
   For this life, you dream of

You dream of a life
That only looks pretty on mannequins

   Mannequins only look good
   Dressed in things you can't afford
   To make you feel inadequate

 you only feel inadequate because
you don't appreciate the life you have

Michael Tavon

Today I Hope

Today I hope,
You rediscover
all the bright
Places inside you,
Since yesterday is a memory
Blown in the wind
And tomorrow
may not meet you halfway
Today is the day
I hope,
You reclaim your bliss
Even if it's for a pocket of time
Savor the present
Before it fades into another
Yesterday,
Before you find yourself
Chasing after
A memory blown in the wind
Today, I hope
You give yourself the chance
To shine again.

Before I Die, I Must Say This

Bodybuilder

I get it,
The weight of life
Gets too heavy to lift alone,
while building the strength
To carry on
You'll find out
Who will spot you
When the burden becomes
Too stressful on your shoulders
True friends
Would never watch you struggle
Without offering a helping hand

Michael Tavon

Greener Grass

If you want greener grass to grow water it with patience and fertilize it with compassion. The grass you have will turn dry if you continue obsessing over the meadows on the other side. It's okay to admire the happiness you desire from afar, but the sun won't shine where bitterness resides. When you see a bed of grass greener than yours, please consider the hours of labor it took for it to rise so radiantly; and aspire to put in the same work. Dreams only bloom into reality when you stop stressing over the grass your neighbors have and focus on watering yours.

Before I Die, I Must Say This

<u>Care 2 Much</u>

They say I care too deeply too soon
and pouring my all into people too early may drown them.
They say my emotions are oceans heavy
 and I need to give people time to stay afloat
I say, being too real reveals who's down for me
I don't need to waste time by toning myself down
I'd rather reveal my true waves
To see who will stay or push me away
Yes, my heart will get submerged in disappointment
But I will always find my way to shore
When I discover who loves me for me
And not the version they expect me to be

Marathon

Life is a marathon,
A search for clarity
But when the finish line is met
And fatigue claims your body
You realize nothing
makes any fucking sense
So why stress over the elements
We can't control

Before I Die, I Must Say This

Wholeness

Wherever you are
I hope love has found its way
To that broken heart of yours
I hope it mends the shattered pieces
So, you can be whole again

Michael Tavon

Feathers I

During a time like this, we must be gentle with each other and ourselves. We must stop chucking stones at feathers and allow each other to be as soft as we need to be. Your heart isn't a brick wall. Let the gardens inside you bloom in every hue. Being vulnerable isn't a curse. Shower the people you care for with compassion when grey clouds pour over their broken hearts. Be gentle with them even when you don't understand. There's no need to slander anyone because you disagree with their stance. It's time to realize you're not always right, and different perspectives can coexist. You'll learn more when you're willing to listen.

Before I Die, I Must Say This

<u>Awareness</u>

Once you reach a heightened level of self-awareness, no one will have the power to break you with cheap words. Low-vibrational insults will no longer seep into your psyche, and what others think of you won't have a chokehold on your mental health. You'll discover a beautiful place inside you and create a home there. Self-awareness is a vital key to inner peace. When you define yourself, no one on this earth will possess the power to tell you who you are.

Fate

You may try to force
The outcome you want
In the end, fate will
Take its course
The universe will always win,
You may not get what you want
But you will always receive
Everything you deserve

Before I Die, I Must Say This

Legacy

When it's all said and done,
What will be the imprint
Left on the surface of this earth by you
What will be your legacy?

Michael Tavon

"Forgive yourself for who you used to be and the mistakes you've made, so your heart can beat softer."

Before I Die, I Must Say This

"Silence often holds more answers
than words. It also provides peace,
when words become too overwhelming
to express."

Michael Tavon

Universal Lessons

Once you start viewing
Your losses as lessons
You'll feel a shift in your perspective

The errors in your ways
Become more clear
So the same actions
Won't repeat when
You dust yourself off
& try again

View your losses as
An opportunity to go back
To the drawing board
Before falling down the rabbit hole
of self-loathing

Sometimes, falling short
is an opportunity to get better

The universe has away
of teaching us lessons through
Heartache and disappointment

Maybe it's a test to see how bad
You want to succeed at the things you love

Before I Die, I Must Say This

Build

Design your happiness
Build your reality
You're the architect
Of your life

Don't let anyone's judgment
Keep you from pursuing your dreams

Bitter people will throw stones
At the house you've built
when you live a life
they don't understand

Michael Tavon

Prism(short): Gatekeepers

Spread,
Your knowledge
Like wings so everyone
Around you can rise high too
Be a vessel of light, not a wall

Before I Die, I Must Say This

Prism: Truth

Guilt
Is a pit
Of rapid quicksand
That will bury you alive
If you refuse to forgive yourself

Lies,
You live by
Flawed mantras to feel safe
Until your sad life becomes
A prophecy of broken promises

Truth,
Is freedom
A safe space on earth
Liberate your heart from shame
Grow from mistakes; your past ain't a grave

Michael Tavon

The Journey

I compete with former versions of myself, no one else. I strive to make my future self smile when he travels to memory lane and realizes how far he's come. My present self celebrates his wins and others as well. The color of envy doesn't touch my golden aura. Time is too precious to waste it on anything that doesn't serve a greater purpose. I forgive who I once was, I'm proud of who I am, and I'm eager to meet the person I'm blooming into.

Before I Die, I Must Say This

Outlook

Once I realize a person is too stubborn to see a perspective outside of their own. I end the conversation before having the last word becomes a never-ending battle. Once my piece has been said, they can waste their breath trying to 'prove me wrong. My outlook is too vivid to waste on dull-minded people.

Michael Tavon

Translucent

I've never been afraid to
Expose my bare truth
for the naked eye to see
Even when amid the darkness
I allow light to pass through -
Giving life to the dead roots inside me

So no matter what others say -
Their bitterness & cruelty
Won't break me

I'm too real with myself
To allow my roots to be
Broken by someone else

Before I Die, I Must Say This

A Special Magic Trick

Depression isn't a magic trick
You can't make it disappear
By pretending it doesn't exist

You create illusions with
The pretty facades you build
But when colors fade
The truth gets revealed

You smile behind smoke & mirrors
When you go outside
~ there's no disguise
To hide the truth that lives inside

Michael Tavon

Anxiety is a Shitty Friend

My day one since daycare,
From every first day of school
To job interview
It's been there,
Second-guessing my every move

A friend by proximity
I keep my anxiety close
Because I fear what
He'd do as an enemy

Anxiety has the loudest whisper
Feeding me the fears
I don't need to hear
It's hard not to listen
When his voice lives in my ear

Anxiety supports my self-esteem
Like a broken crutch
It only comes to see me fall
Then plays a requiem for my broken dream

Anxiety is a shitty friend,
When I swim in self-doubt
He watches me drown
without lending a hand
Yet, I still keep him around

Before I Die, I Must Say This

Section III: Before I Die

Michael Tavon

If pain is weakness leaving the body, does that make me stronger for loving you despite being pushed away time and time again?

Before I Die, I Must Say This

Heart/Break

Give your heart a rest; you carry too much stress on those shoulders. The toxic people you love are burdens blinding you with a smile, so the red flags seem blurry. They latch onto your goodwill because you're afraid to say no; you treat yourself like an afterthought. Give your heart a rest before it implodes. Give your heart a break before your mind breaks down. Choosing yourself is never selfish. If their love for you is genuine, they will understand.

Michael Tavon

Before I Die, I Must Say This I

I'm tired of apologizing for
Not being the version of myself
You want me to be,

See, rivers too deep
for most to swim in
flow through this heart of mine
And my mind travels to places
Most people can't fathom

Which means I'm not going
To remain the same
stop comparing me
To who I used to be
that person is long gone

Who I am today,
Is someone
worth getting to know
Just give me a chance

If I was able to let go of my past
What's holding you back from
Accepting the person I am today?

Before I Die, I Must Say This

Eye Contact

When she gazes
Into the windows of my soul
she speaks a language
Without saying a word
My heart, entranced
By her telepathy
I feel at home when she
Stares at me
Amid the bliss of silence
Sparks fly from my iris
Because love lives in her eyes

Michael Tavon

Secrets

If my darkest secrets
were to ever come to light
Would you still love me the same
Or would shame
be synonymous with my name
Whenever you stare into my
mournful eyes?

Before I Die, I Must Say This

No one in this world
Makes me feel safer
more warm – less lonely
 & more loved than you
That's why I call you home

Michael Tavon

the love we share is a tranquil home
that keeps us safe from the storms
that try to tear us apart.

Before I Die, I Must Say This

Connected

A connection isn't measured
By the distance
Between two souls
When they're oceans apart

It's the closeness they feel
Even when their eyes don't meet
Face to face

See, some couples sleep
In the same bed, but still feel
Like they're dreaming next to a stranger

While long-distance lovers
Grow closer through facetime sessions
And love notes

Being aligned with a heart
Mountains apart
is beauty symmetry

you don't have to settle for someone
because of proximity,
There is no zip code attached to love

Michael Tavon

Connected II:

Falling for someone via tweets and glass screens was once deemed taboo and farfetched. With this world being more connected than ever, possibilities have become endless. Your soulmate may live by mountains while you're shading under palm trees. When you open your heart to the world outside of your hometown, you will find happiness in the places you least expect. The universe has a way of presenting the colors your mind was too grey to see when you explore life outside the norm.

Before I Die, I Must Say This

Shield

Sometimes I just want
to wrap my arms around
your body so tight,
it forms a barrier between
you and the grief
That shrouds you

Michael Tavon

Heartbroken Clouds

Something must've broken your heart
Why else are you sobbing and grey
Darkness fills the sky
After a long day -
your are left to grieve alone
Endless tears,
Become tiny ponds
On concrete grounds
another lonely night
For the heartbroken cloud
You want to be loved
But you can only be loved from afar
Raindrops of sorrow
I blow a kiss to the sky
And for pray the clouds
To feel better tomorrow

Before I Die, I Must Say This

The Night Makes Beautiful Music

Slide the window open,
 so the cold autumn air can
welcome itself to our room

Draw the curtain back,
to hear the rain sing in falsetto
to a beautiful tune

The nighttime makes beautiful music
When I'm next to you

I wrap my arm around your body -
You rest half nude

I wish you'd stay up with me -
You drift into your dreams too soon

This weather is melatonin
to a restless mind

Meditative rainfall,
calm noise, when I close my eyes

Michael Tavon

Complete Love

I was whole before we met; somehow, she found new ways to complete me. Her presence became a safe space for me to be free. Falling for her wasn't an extreme sport. Giving my heart to her wasn't a gamble. The way constellations on her face light ups when she exposes her gap-toothed smile is the prettiest sight my eyes have been blessed to behold. She took this love and made it synonymous with bliss. I was complete before we met, but having her in my life helped me see how love feels when the soul is free from the chains of loneliness and confusion.

Before I Die, I Must Say This

Goodnight, I love you

We spell "goodnight.'
With our lips,
and say, "I love you" -
Like a mantra.
Before the curtains
Of our eyes close,
And sweet dreams eagerly await for us
To meet them halfway.
The slight space between us
Becomes a haven under silk sheets
My armrests on your hip
My hand finds comfort on your thigh
your warmth is my melatonin
I catch z's the way
newborns do -
Unbothered by the madness
Happening outside,
I'm blessed to have
My nights end with you

Michael Tavon

Gardens

I plant my lips to
your forehead,
whenever thoughts of you
Bloom into my mind

Before I Die, I Must Say This

Architects

Let's build a love
taller than skyscrapers,
So, we can feel
the clouds between our fingertips

With all we have
 let's match each other's efforts
to build a home together.

Michael Tavon

Note to an Old Friend:

Forgiveness is not a sign of weakness, nor is it a permission slip to give you access to my space again. You've crossed a sacred boundary with no regard too many times. There's no coming back from that. I'll hold myself accountable for making you feel empowered enough to treat me like dirt.
I've evolved from the fool who was colorblind to the red flags you wore. The space between you and me provided clarity. Now I see who you are and who you've always been. I forgive, but I still don't fuck with you.

Before I Die, I Must Say This

<u>Dodging a Bullet</u>

Loving you was a bullet I was willing to take
By grace, you spared my life
When you chose not to pull the trigger,
Thank you for not reciprocating
The feelings I had for you
Now I can live to love another day
So fuck you, don't ever walk into my life again.

Michael Tavon

To My First Heartbreak

After the last drop fell from my cloudy eyes
I began to realize the heartbreak you gave
Was the biggest blessing my soul craved
When you pushed me away
I was given the space
To remember who I used to be
Before losing myself
Within the image
You designed for me to be

Before I Die, I Must Say This

Please, don't say you miss me after you spent so much time pushing me away.

Michael Tavon

Skipping Stones

like stones on a pond
my heart skips a beat
when she smiles at me

Before I Die, I Must Say This

Wealth

This world is so corrupted,
Our character is built through suffering

our strength is defined
by the amount of suffering we survive

If grief and despair gets spent like currency,
What's your net worth currently?

I'd go broke for a smile
And little joy to make life worthwhile

I wish happiness
was worth as much as gold
Too bad it's worthless
In this sad, cold world

Michael Tavon

Sleep: Death

They say sleep
is the cousin a death for a reason
I stayed up until five am,
Maybe, I feared dying in my sleep

Too many nights when gunshots blasted
like bass through subwoofers
I awoke out of deep slumber

Fear made me restless
I didn't want to become another casualty
I rejected sleep,
Like an overtired toddler

If a wild bullet invited himself
Through my door, wall, or windows
At least, I'd see him coming

If I never die in my dreams,
I won't die if I'm not sleeping
was my logic

Sleep has no peace
A piece of steel welcomes death at night,

A nocturnal being I had become
I was afraid to lose my life
In my sleep

Before I Die, I Must Say This

Prism: Sleep

Sleep,
Come near me
This temple needs you
To buy me more time on earth
I don't want to die tired, broken

Rest,
My strained eyes
Close like traffic doors
idle thoughts become patrons
Late-night rush, I'd die to feel alive

Dreams,
From slumber
In a restless bed
Im'a leave this earth tired,
At least, sleep will find me six feet deep

Michael Tavon

Before I Die, I Must Say This II

I will always love you,
Let my heart be a vessel
Of transparency - A space
where you flow like the river
you were born to be

You don't have
To carry your burdens alone
There's no mountain
I wouldn't move with you

So come as you are,
What's gold will last forever
Even when I'm long gone
We will share an unbreakable bond

Spread your light in all its glory,
Thank you for
Allowing me to play a special part
In your story

Before I Die, I Must Say This

Dis(Connected)

Long after you were gone
Your seven digits + area code
Was locked —safe
In case you wanted to see
If my number remained the same,
It never changed,
The same way my feelings
for you never did,

For each passing moon
And rising sun
The hope I held so near to my heart,
Slowly slipped out of my hands
I wanted nothing more
Than a *hey* or *how you've been*
 To see if you had
an ounce of care to spare

Over time your name
became synonymous
With radio silence
Since every sad song
reminded me of you,

Through loneliness, I began
To appreciate heartache.
In your absence
I forgot how to miss you

When you tried to reconnect
I was strong enough
To tell you to fuck off.

Michael Tavon

Dead Butterflies

Missing someone you still love
Is an illness that kills all the butterflies
In your stomach
You try to heal with time
And medicate with the vices
You self-prescribe
Yet the black hole still resides inside
You begin to feel weak, worthless
Void of purpose
Wondering how love could hurt like this
As the pieces mend
You can no longer ignore
What they never did
You can't pretend
They didn't break you
Until you were shallow thin
Causing the illness –
You had to heal from alone

Before I Die, I Must Say This

Talk it Out III

Let's settle the tension between
Between you & I
Before we rest tonight
Our bond is too strong
To sleep
With angry hearts and teary eyes

Speak your truth
So I can hear your point of view
 set your pride to the side
And listen to how I feel too

Stop pointing fingers,
The blame game
Never ends with a winner
Don't let the bitter feelings linger
I hope you reconsider,
See things clearer

Before we kiss
the moon goodnight,
Let's talk it out
Until we understand
each other's side

Michael Tavon

To the One I Love

This love feels so good
I pinch myself to make sure it's real

As the hands of time
Stretch from side to side
I cherish each moment we share

Since all good things come to an end
I must savor our time together
In case the curtain close between us

til death do us part
Becomes a broken promise
In most fairy tales

The reality is I will love you
With all I have, as long as you do the same

I hope you have the patience
to forgive me when I fuck up
I pray for clarity between the blurred lines

I don't know
If it's arrogance or naivety
But all lovers believe their love
Is something that will pass
The test of time

Before I Die, I Must Say This

One thing I do know
As long the butterflies
Float inside you, and I
We will share
One gorgeous life

Michael Tavon

Love is(n't)

Love isn't immersing
Your soul into their world
So profoundly, you lose the essence
Of who you are

Love isn't the glue that will
Mend your broken heart

Love isn't a drug
Your body depends on
When life gets dark

Love isn't a war
That leaves wounds & scars

If you think love is a crutch
You lean on 'cause you dread being lonely
you're falling in love
for all the wrong reasons

Love is the contradiction
To the aforementioned

It's where two different worlds meet
Without collision

Love is a beautiful cult of two or
A few – with no hearts codependent

Before I Die, I Must Say This

Love is a garden
Where new life blooms
Under the sun & sky blue

Above all, love is the
Peace you come home to
When the world is at war against you

Michael Tavon

Crybaby

Give a toddler
An expensive toy
They treat it like trash

Give them a spatula
Watch them wave it like
a magic wand
as their laughter
fills the atmosphere

When you pry that spatula
From their little palm
Joy turns to grief in a heartbeat
They cry from the depths
of their belly
Until you give it back

Babies don't see price tags
They fall in love with
The simplistic beauty life has to offer

Adults lose the ability
to be enticed by
the mundane,
the moment we become
Vanity slaves

Before I Die, I Must Say This

3:21 am: Rest In Peace

My eyes
slowly drift shut
I resist a Benadryl slumber.
As my dreams beg me
to meet them halfway,
I'm too stubborn
To say goodnight to the moon.
I prefer to stay awake
Til the sun says good morning

I treat sleep like
it's a waste of time
30 years young,
Fighting rest
Like a toddler,
What am I so afraid to miss?

Maybe I'm afraid of my dreams coming true
& this is my way of running away from them

Michael Tavon

I write to live
I live to write.

Before I Die, I Must Say This

College

Someone once asked
"Why don't you go to school for writing."

I was livid,
 Why pay someone
 To teach me what's God-given
 All these sonnets in my soul
 My heart beats in limericks

Part of me thought
 it was degrading
 to be graded,
 On something other
 than science and equations
 Instead of being a desk slave
 I avoided the majors

I knew being a student of life
 Would help hone my craft
 Better than any class
 when I dropped out of college
 To become a writer
 my family didn't understand

Now, I ain't knocking
 Those who go to college
 To acquire the knowledge
 It's just my logic

Michael Tavon

I didn't need anyone
With a degree
Telling me how stories
and poetry should be,
art with no apologies
I create to be free

Before I Die, I Must Say This

My Approach to Life the Same as Writing

If I don't discover new ways
to better myself
I'm wasting my time.

If I don't stop pressuring myself to be perfect,
I will never be satisfied.

I desire to grow
and help others heal
Along the way,

Let my heart beat
At an easy pace
This isn't a race,
There's no need to rush
Take it day by day

Travel far and often
Before time is gone
Your perspective changes
When you see the world outside
Of your own

Always be a student,
To enhance your mind

Some days may feel like hell
But heaven is never hard to find

Never be complacent
Pursue every passion

Michael Tavon

Be a man of my word
Don't be all talk
Prove with action

Before I Die, I Must Say This

To the Teachers I Loved

To Mrs. Martin
The one who saw
The hidden diamonds
Inside this soul of mine
And gave me the confidence
to let them shine.
You knew I was a rare jewel
Trying to fit into a world
of coal and rubble
You told me I would never shine
if I kept hiding from the sun

To Ms. Cooper,
The personification of cool
With locs that swing gracefully
Like tree vine
Your class was like a sip
Of caramel mocha in the morning
You'd dance in front of the class to
smooth jazz & Prince
as we recited Maya Angelou and
 Langston Hughes
Your classroom - a spoken word lounge
And I discovered my fondness for poetry
Because of you
Thank you for sparking
The light in me to write.

Michael Tavon

To Mrs. Wright,
You exuded passion
From your pores
And it rubbed off on your students
I fell in love with the stage
You encouraged me to step
Into the spotlight and make it mine
You saw my gift and said,
"it would be a waste if I kept it to myself."

To the great teachers
Please be aware,
You do make a difference,
Every day you teach a young mind
You are changing a life.

Before I Die, I Must Say This

The Poem I'd Write for YOU If I Were Joe Goldberg

I wanna get to know you the way
Your diary knows your truth
Look into my eyes,
Show me your mirror's
Point of view
Treat me like your bed too,
Lay your body onto me
So I can fade into you

Tell me everything your walls know,
With me, your secrets will never get exposed
Open up to me,
There's no need to keep your heart closed

Let me learn the real you :

The version of you very few know
Tell me how you like your coffee
& which detergent do you use
to clean your clothes

I wanna know the real you,
From your birth chart to your favorite
Song lyric, tell me the story behind
Your first piecing I promise I'll listen

Let me learn the real you
So I can fall in love with everything you are
Not the thought of you
Or a façade

Michael Tavon

Adulthood

Growing up,
Adult life seemed like receiving
A pack of white socks
On Christmas Day -
Practical,
but nothing to be excited about

With the burden of living in adult flesh
The scent of Ben Gay
was my oldhead's cologne
Carrying all that stress
Left them with brittles knees
& a spine knotted like shoelaces

Adults traded candy & kool-aid
For cigarettes & Hennessy
To find some type of peace

Timeout and detention
Became handcuff and penitentiary's
When they made terrible decisions

When adults went
k-i-s-s-i-n-g in a tree
the baby carriage
Came before love
Then came marriage
Followed by years of being average

The adults I knew
Didn't work their dreams jobs
Which gave me little hope as a child

Before I Die, I Must Say This

Adults played *eeny meeny miny* moe
Between paying the car note or keeping
The water on

Being an adult never seemed
Glamorous from my point of view
In hindsight,
I'm happy I didn't grow up too soon

Michael Tavon

Unfinished Poems

Digging my own grave,
Plot 6 feet of dark emptiness
I'll bury the shame
That burdens my flesh,

The guilt that pumps through
My blood will cease to flow
I want to be free- let go
I lack self-control

The whispers scream so loud
I yearn to indulge

Before I Die, I Must Say This

Puppetmaster

I don't wish for us to go back to normal,
my hope for us is to go back to *natural*.

We've been controlled like puppets
far too long
We've forgotten who we truly are

Humans have been brainwashed
To believe suppressing your feelings
Is normal, and slaving for 40 + hours
a week is the only way to survive.

We were raised to be ashamed of our sexual urges, and
without money our lives are worthless.

There's nothing normal about
Working from sunrise til darkness falls
There's nothing normal about
Drinking milk from a cow
There's nothing normal
About a mother going back to work
Weeks after giving birth to her child

But we've been brainwashed
To believe this is the way life
is supposed to be

We've been trained to not think critically

Michael Tavon

Being a human being is such a scary thing

There's nothing natural about being normal
And being normal ain't natural

We're all dangling by the strings
Controlled by this mysterious puppet master

Before I Die, I Must Say This

Lost in The Mundane

The grief felt from dreams deferred and suppressed desires will manifest into the regrets that'll turn our hairs grey before we become of old age.

Since we only get one chance to live in this present body, pursue every experience your heart craves, chase every dream your mind envisions.

Don't get so lost in the mundane that you forget how extraordinary you are. Life is what you make it make sure it's the life you'll be proud of when it's all said & done.

Michael Tavon

I fear the what if's. My mind is filled with all the if's one brain can store. I fear the unknown and every tomorrow. Most of all, I fear disappointing the people who believe in me.

Before I Die, I Must Say This

Give yourself the flowers you deserve

Michael Tavon

The End

Printed in Great Britain
by Amazon